Teaching Primary Science
OUTDOORS!

by Helen Spring

Millgate House Education

The **Association**
for **Science Education**
Promoting Excellence in Science Teaching and Learning

Copyright © Millgate House Publishers 2021

First published 2021 by Millgate House Publishers.

Millgate House Publishers is an imprint of
Millgate House Education Ltd
A publishing arm of
The Association for Science Education
College Lane
Hatfield
AL10 9AA

The right of Helen Spring to be identified as the author of this work has been asserted in accordance with the Copyright, Designs and Patent Act 1988.

Typesetting and Graphic Design by Jo Williams

Stock images courtesy of Shutterstock and Pixabay

Printed and bound in Great Britain by Ashford Colour Press

ISBN 978-0-86357-473-3

British Library Cataloguing in Publication Data

A catalogue record for this book is available from the British Library

Acknowledgements

Many people have helped me to write the lesson plans in this book. I would like to thank everyone who has trialled my lesson plans, suggested ideas and given constructive criticism. I'd also like to thank the teachers and friends who have provided photographs of children and examples of their work.

Particular thanks to my fellow PSQM hub leaders Nicki Deane, Kathryn Horan, Leigh Hoath, Mandy Hodgskinson and Claire Davies for their support, as well as to the following teachers and friends (and their children) for their contributions: Julie Wistow, Bernadette Chernenko, Joanne Cantello, Molly Moss, Bev Watson, Becky Salisbury and Jenny Flude. Thanks also to all at Howsham Mill and to Jennifer Duncan for her photography skills.

Special thanks go to Jo Williams and Pat Spring (my mum!) for their proofreading and editing skills.

Thank you for reading my book!

Helen Spring

Contents

Table of activities

Introduction

Instinctively, most of us know that being outdoors is good for us in some way. The fact that you're reading this book suggests that you see the value in teaching and learning outdoors! This brief summary should support you in identifying research to back up that intuitive feeling.

There is a wealth of research which highlights the health benefits of simply being outdoors (Twohig-Bennett and Jones, 2018); this includes research that suggests that being in green spaces in childhood is associated with lower risk of psychiatric disorders later in life (Engemann et al, 2019). Learning outdoors has also been found to have a positive impact on pupils' and teachers' health and wellbeing (Waite et al, 2016).

As teachers and educators, our job is about more than improving children's health and wellbeing. Primarily, we want to raise children's academic attainment and performance. Adventure learning outdoors can accelerate children's progress (Education Endowment Foundation, 2021). It would seem that non-cognitive skills such as perseverance and resilience are developed through adventure learning and that these skills have a knock-on impact on academic outcomes. Learning maths outdoors can also significantly impact on the amount of academic progress children make (Harvey et al, 2017). Children have also been found to perform better at tasks in outdoor settings and to have superior recollection (Hamilton, 2018). This is attributed to increased opportunities for group work.

Most teachers will be able to say, anecdotally, that children are happier when learning outdoors. Waite et al (2016) found that children enjoyed learning outdoors and were more engaged in outdoor settings. Waite et al make the link between engagement and motivation, arguing that this is because learning outdoors fosters a love of learning, encourages pupils to enjoy the learning process and offers a different way of learning that is perceived as fun and gives purpose to learning.

Several studies have linked improvements in behaviour to learning outdoors – this is often attributed to children having more opportunities to collaborate and interact with other children outdoors (Waite et al, 2016; Hamilton, 2018; and Dowdell et al, 2011). Ofsted (2008) have also discussed how learning outside the classroom can contribute towards raising standards and improving pupils' personal, social and emotional development.

When children learn outdoors, they have greater confidence in their own abilities; this means that they feel able to try different challenges within and outside the classroom (Waite et al, 2016). The effect of outdoor learning on children's self-confidence is particularly notable for underachieving pupils, whose contribution and self-confidence matches that of their peers when learning outdoors (Hamilton, 2018).

There are clearly many opportunities for teaching primary science outdoors, and some aspects of primary science are better taught outdoors because children are able to see how science is relevant to their lives and the world beyond school (Harlen and Qualter, 2014).

It is always important to consider Health and Safety when teaching science – whether indoors or outdoors. The ASE's *Be Safe!* can be a useful starting point, as can membership of CLEAPSS.

You need to check out the learning environment before going outdoors. See especially *Be Safe!* 4th edition 2011, sections 6, pages 12-14. Look for broken glass (and clear it away safely), fouling by dogs and cats, stinging nettles, poisonous plants, etc.

Be prepared for emergencies, e.g. with no dust pan and brush available or no fire extinguishers, how will you deal with broken glass when using glass containers or ensure that a fire can be safely put out?

Throughout this book, notes about health and safety have been made, but it is important to risk assess for your own setting and cohort.

Other barriers commonly cited are children's behaviour, staffing and resources. The majority of lessons in this book require only the types of resources that most schools already have, and may be used more commonly indoors. Effective planning and preparation for learning outdoors may alleviate the need for additional staffing, but, again, this is something that is unique to every school. In order to ensure that any lesson – including lessons taught outdoors – is effective and covers the objectives intended, it is necessary to spend time planning and preparing. Key points to consider when teaching outdoors should include:

- How will you support children in making the transitions from within the classroom to beyond it?

- Can you ensure both regular and frequent use of the outdoor setting?

- How will you prepare children for working in the outdoors? Consider how to address the basic psychological and physiological needs of the children before leaving the classroom.

- How will you manage the transition back to the classroom?

- What are your expectations with regards to dialogue between children and between the teacher and children?

(Adapted from Hoath (2015).

How to use this book

Each activity in this book provides the following information:

- **Age range** – For which age group is the lesson suitable?

- **Enquiry type** – Which of the 5 types of enquiry is used in this lesson? Further guidance about the 5 types of enquiry can be found in the book *It's Not Fair - or is it?* (Millgate House Education 2011).

- **Topic title**

- **Conceptual knowledge** – Lesson objectives that support children's acquisition of knowledge.

- **Working scientifically** – Lesson objectives that support the development of scientific enquiry skills.

- **Assessment** – A description of what children meeting the objectives will be able to do.

- **Resources needed** – What equipment will need to be prepared in advance of the lesson?

- **What to do** – Ideas for how to structure the lesson.

- **Assessment for learning** – Formative assessment activities that can take place as part of the lesson; these can be used to inform future teaching.

- **Science Capital** – Suggested ideas for developing children's Science Capital as part of the lesson, or as an addition to the lesson. Further guidance about the Science Capital Teaching Approach can be found in the downloadable resources.

- **Support** – Guidance for supporting children who are working below age-related expectations.

- **Extension** – Guidance for challenging more able children.

- **Follow up** – Suggested ideas for follow-up lessons.

- **Key vocabulary**

- **Download resources and links for this activity** – This section will include external links as well as any worksheets or other resources created for *Teaching Primary Science Outdoors*.

1. Plants

Conceptual knowledge

In this activity, children identify and describe the basic structure of a variety of common flowering plants, including trees.

Working scientifically

In this activity, children observe closely, using simple equipment.

Assessment

Children meeting the conceptual knowledge objective will be able to identify the parts of a plant. They will be able to verbally describe the different parts of a plant.

Children meeting the working scientifically objective will be able to use a magnifying glass correctly and verbally describe what they can see.

Activity - Identifying parts of a plant

Resources needed

Trowels or spades with which to dig up plants or plants that have already been dug up.
Magnifying glasses
Labels for part of a plant (if desired)

What to do

Take the children for a short walk to look for plants. Discuss how trees, grasses and shrubs are plants too. Children often hold the misconception that a plant is a flower, or that all flowers are brightly coloured. Draw their attention to grass flowers (florets) and trees to help address these misconceptions.

Depending on your context, provide the children with trowels or spades and ask them to dig up a plant. Alternatively, bring some plants with you (pansies are usually quite cheap from garden centres/supermarkets). It is important that plants still have their roots so that the children can see them.

Ask the children to work in groups to identify different parts of a plant. You may wish to provide them with labels to identify the different parts of the plant. These could include leaf, flower, petal, root, stem, stalk and bud. Get them to use a magnifying glass to look closely at the plants. You may need to give guidance on how to use the magnifying glass – many children hold the glass up to their eye rather than up to the object they are looking at. Children can then describe what they can see through the magnifying glass.

Find a plant or tree and discuss the parts of the plant or the tree. Depending on the time of year, this would include the leaf, flower, blossom, petal, fruit, berry, root, seed, trunk, branch, bark and bud.

Ensure that children wash their hands thoroughly after working outdoors.

Assessment for Learning

Ask the children to use environmental art (see picture) to represent the parts of a plant. They could say how their picture is like a real plant and how it is different. You may wish to provide labels for the parts of a plant, or you may wish to simply ask the child to identify and describe the different parts of the plant to you. The children could take part in an outdoor environmental art exhibition where they show other children their artwork and identify the different parts of a plant. You could photograph the environmental art, with or without labels, and these photographs could be stuck into the children's workbooks. If labels have not been used outdoors, you could ask the children to label the photograph.

Use this task to identify any misconceptions that you can address in future lessons.

Science Capital

Ask the children whether they grow plants at home. Find out if the people they live with work with plants. Discuss jobs that involve plants, such as gardener, botanist and countryside ranger.

Support

Some children may need support to use a magnifying glass. Model how to do it – use a larger magnifying glass.

Extension

To add extra challenge for more able children, provide a range of equipment for them to choose from. This might include a magnifying glass, microscope, binoculars, pooter, etc.

Follow up

Children can label a diagram showing the parts of a plant.

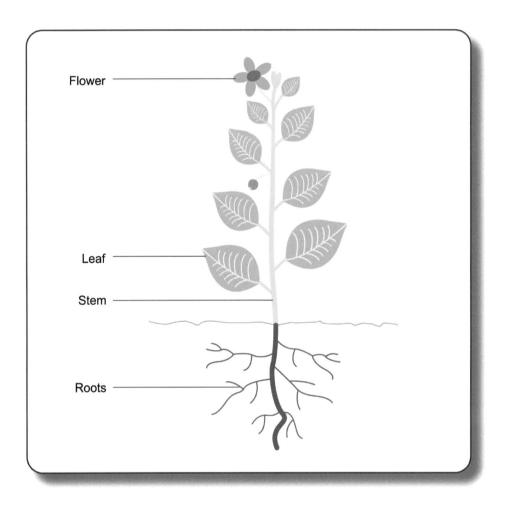

Key vocabulary

Leaf, flower, blossom, petal, fruit, berry, root, seed, trunk, branch, stem, bark, stalk, bud
Names of trees in the local area
Names of garden and wild flowering plants in the local area

Download resources and links @ www.millgatehouse.co.uk/tpsoresources

2. Animals including humans

Conceptual knowledge

In this activity, children identify, name, draw and label the basic parts of the human body and say which part of the body is associated with each sense.

Working scientifically

In this activity, children identify which part of the body is associated with each sense.

Assessment

Children meeting the conceptual knowledge objective will be able to correctly suggest things that they can see, hear, touch and smell. In conversation, they will be able to name the associated body parts.

Children meeting the working scientifically objective will be able to identify the parts of the body associated with each sense and to identify what each sense is.

Activity - Using the senses

Resources needed

Sensory memory box worksheet (see downloads)
Pens/pencils or double-sided sticky tape if sticking things on
Clipboards

What to do

Discuss senses with the children. Ask them which part of the body they use to see, to hear, to taste, to touch and to smell.

Depending on responses, you may wish to use examples from the outdoor environment to demonstrate/reinforce these concepts, for example, touching moss and a tree trunk to feel the difference between hard and soft, listening for bird song, looking for colours, or smelling flowers.

Taste is a difficult sense to explore in the outdoor setting unless you have ready access to blackberries or similar. However, if you do eat wild berries, ensure that you reinforce health and safety guidance with children – never eat anything that you find growing outdoors unless an adult has said that it's safe to do so. You may wish to bring some snacks outdoors to taste, or this may be something that you follow up indoors.

Ask the children to find a quiet space and consider what they can see, hear, touch and smell. Use the worksheet provided if it is helpful. It could be used to support writing in the classroom afterwards. The worksheet can be completed using words, pictures or sticking items on to the sheet (use double-sided sticky tape for this).

Ensure children wash their hands thoroughly after working outdoors.

Assessment for Learning

Ask the children what they can see, hear, touch and smell. If necessary, prompt them with examples of your own. Ask the children which part of the body is associated with each of these senses. Where they are unsure, you will need to revisit the lesson objectives. Get children to explore their senses one at a time, for example, if they close their eyes, ask them what they can hear. With their hands over their ears, ask them what they can see.

Science Capital

Ask the children what they can hear and smell at home. Draw on any experiences such as living near a farm, takeaway or busy road. Discuss what can be heard, seen and smelt in the local area – the brewery, the hills, the birds, etc. Consider how senses are used in children's everyday lives: Do any of the children, or their family members, read braille? Is there a crossing near school that beeps?

Discuss jobs that involve using senses, such as a sound engineer or nutritionist.

Support

Provide pictures of the parts of the body associated with each sense (see downloads).

Extension

To challenge more able children, give them a blank piece of paper rather than a worksheet, and ask them to record what they experience through their senses.

Follow up

Give children an image of the human body and ask them to annotate it to show which parts of the body are associated with which sense. This could also be done by laying string around a child to get the shape and then adding sticky note labels onto an upside-down flower pot and using them to mark the body parts associated with the senses. Alternatively, they could stick the labels on one of their classmates. You might also want to play a game of 'Simon Says' outside, where the children point to different parts of the body associated with senses.

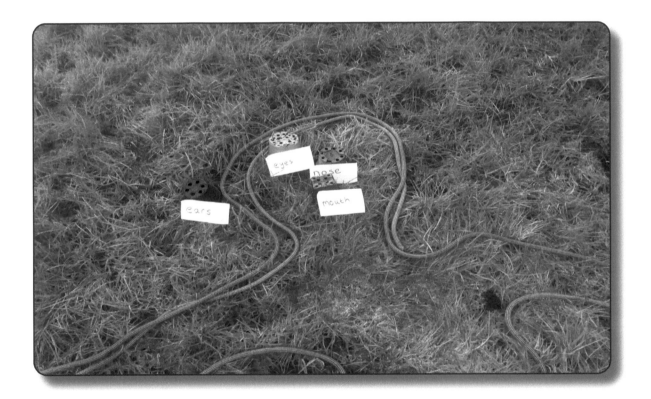

Key vocabulary

Senses, touch, see, smell, taste, hear, fingers (skin), eyes, nose, ear, tongue

Download resources and links @ www.millgatehouse.co.uk/tpsoresources

3. Uses of everyday materials

Conceptual knowledge

In this activity, children distinguish between an object and the material from which it is made, and identify and name a variety of everyday materials, including wood, plastic, glass, metal, water, and rock.

Working scientifically

In this activity, children identify different types of materials.

Assessment

Children meeting the conceptual knowledge objectives will be able to say what an object is and what material it is made from. They will be able to identify and name a number of different materials.

Children meeting the working scientifically objective will be able to identify a number of different materials. Children will need further work to ensure that they are secure with classifying materials.

Activity - Identifying and naming materials

Resources needed

Depending on your setting and context, you may need to set out some objects in advance of the lesson. These are not limited to, but might include:

PE equipment made of wood, plastic and metal

Cups made of plastic, glass and paper. Care should be taken to supervise children around the glass cup and be prepared in case it gets broken

Spoons made of metal, wood and plastic

Something made of rock – e.g. garden ornament, gravel, jewellery, brick, paperweight

What to do

Start by taking the children outdoors to look for objects made of different materials. This might include looking at a shed made of wood or metal, play equipment, usually made of wood or metal, signs made of plastic or metal, rails or fences made of different materials, things in the school garden, etc.

Address the fact that (for example) the shed is made of wood, but not all sheds are made of wood. You may also wish to start discussing properties of materials.

Call out a material (wood, plastic, metal, glass, water, rock – more if appropriate). Ask the children to find an object made of that material (use the words 'object' and 'material'). Depending on your setting and context, you may be able to ask the children to go to the object and identify it, or you may wish to ask them to bring items to you.

Ensure that children wash their hands thoroughly after working outdoors.

Assessment for Learning

Ask the children to tell you what the object is that they have found (e.g. tennis racquet) and what it is made from (e.g. metal and plastic). Ask if the object could be made of any other material. For example, a table tennis bat might be made of wood or plastic.

If the children are not sure of the names of different materials, you may need to revisit the lesson objectives by exploring the school grounds and introducing them to a range of different objects made from particular materials (e.g. a wooden fence, a wooden climbing frame and a wooden door).

Science Capital

Using objects and materials that children are familiar with or that are in their local environment will help to develop Science Capital. Ask the children if they have objects made from different materials in their homes (what is made from wood in your home?). Find out if any of the children have family members who use materials in their work or as a hobby, such as a joiner, carpenter or metal fabricator.

Support

Provide the children with an example of the raw material, such as a block of wood or a plastic cube.

Extension

To add extra challenge for more able children, increase the range of materials that they have to identify and name.

Follow up

Take a photograph of the objects that the children looked at. Ask them to annotate the photograph to identify the different materials that they can see.

Key vocabulary

Object, material, wood, plastic, glass, metal, water, rock, brick, paper, fabric, elastic, foil, card/cardboard, rubber, wool, clay, hard, soft, stretchy, stiff, bendy, floppy

Download resources and links @ www.millgatehouse.co.uk/tpsoresources

4. Seasonal changes

Conceptual knowledge

In this activity, children observe and describe weather associated with the seasons.

Working scientifically

In this activity, children gather and record data to help in answering questions.

Assessment

Children meeting the conceptual knowledge objectives will be able to observe and describe the weather at different times of year. They may be able to write this down, draw pictures to indicate this, or simply explain the different types of weather that they have observed.

Children meeting the working scientifically objective will be able to gather and record data such as wind speed or amount of water. They will be able to use this data to answer questions such as 'which season is the rainiest?'

Activity - Observing and describing the weather

Resources needed

To make a rain gauge, you will need a plastic bottle, a marker pen, a ruler and some scissors
To make a wind speed gauge, you will need a paper plate or some cardboard, some string, scissors and a felt tip pen
Any equipment in school for measuring the weather such as data loggers, thermometers or a weather station

What to do

Seasonal change cannot be taught well in a block. It is a topic that needs teaching and revisiting throughout the year. Ideally, children should go outdoors weekly and discuss the weather. If there is unusual weather, such as snow, the children should be given the opportunity to experience it first-hand.

Prior to going outdoors, the children need to make gauges with which to measure the weather. Alternatively, you may have these ready-made. You may also have equipment in school for measuring the weather. This might include data loggers, which can record the amount of light, thermometers or weather stations.

Ideally, the children should be involved in designing the equipment – the scale on the gauges does not need to be using a formal unit of measurement – in fact it might even read 'not windy, a little bit windy and very windy'.

Using the equipment available, the children go outdoors at various points in the year to measure rainfall, temperature and wind speed. You might also ask them to describe the weather.

The children need to record the data they collect – this might be in a table or on a tablet. You might want them to record their findings on a whiteboard outdoors, and then complete a table back in the classroom. There are many opportunities here for cross-curricular links with maths.

It can be helpful to have an ongoing interactive display relating to the weather throughout the seasons. This might take the form of a wall display, audio diary or photo journal.

Ensure that children wash their hands thoroughly after working outdoors.

Assessment for Learning

Ask the children to tell you what the weather is like and what season it is. How is the weather different in other seasons? Children may have the misconception, for example, that it always snows in winter. If this is the case, they could carry out research into when it has snowed in the UK, or in their local area, and how often it really snows.

Ask the children what data they need to collect about the weather and what this data will tell them. Use their answers to inform planning. Children may need to develop their understanding of different weather types and how we might go about measuring the weather.

Science Capital

Regularly visiting somewhere in the local area will help to develop children's Science Capital. Discuss things which are personal to the children – what coat are they wearing and why, who has had to put sun cream on, etc. Talk about people whose jobs involve knowing about seasons, such as farmers, climatologists and ecologists. Consider also jobs such as air traffic controllers and fishing boat crew.

Support

Provide the children with pictures of different weather types, which they can assign to different days/seasons (see downloads).

Extension

To add extra challenge for more able children, ask them to take readings from a thermometer or data logger using standard units.

Follow up

Ask the children to use environmental art to represent the seasons and/or write a poem about each of the seasons.

Key vocabulary

Weather (sunny, rainy, windy, snowy, etc.), seasons (winter, summer, spring, autumn), Sun, sunrise, sunset, day length

Download resources and links @ www.millgatehouse.co.uk/tpsoresources

5. Living things and their habitats

Conceptual knowledge

In this activity, children identify that most living things live in habitats to which they are suited and describe how different habitats provide for the basic needs of different kinds of animals and plants, and how they depend on each other. Children also identify and name a variety of plants and animals in their habitats, including microhabitats.

Working scientifically

In this activity, children observe closely, using simple equipment.

Assessment

Children meeting the conceptual knowledge objective will be able to correctly name the living thing that they have found. The address that they write will include a description of the habitat. Any writing or discussion should ideally include how the habitat provides food, shelter, air, water and space.

Children meeting the working scientifically objective will be able to use the equipment provided to observe living things. You may wish to ask children to draw a scientific drawing of the living thing(s) that they find.

Activity - Identifying and describing habitats

Resources needed

Identification sheets or identification books
Pooters or bug collectors, and magnifying glasses (See *Be Safe!*, Section 6, page 13 for guidance on cleaning pooters)
Apps such as Pl@ntnet that help to identify plants
Handheld microscope if available
Camera
Clipboards
Pencils
Postcard-sized pieces of cardboard/blank postcards

What to do

Show the children how to use the equipment provided. Set any other health and safety guidance needed. Depending on your location, this may include being careful to avoid dog mess, not touching rubbish, or avoiding stinging nettles.

Give the children time to explore their environment and find a selection of minibeasts and plants. They should identify and name these and make a note of where they were found (their habitat). You may want to take photographs (or get the children to take photographs) of what they have found.

The children then write a 'habitat postcard', which includes the 'address' of the living thing – encourage them to put as much description in here as they can, e.g.:

Mr S Slug
Under the wet leaves
Next to the tree stump
School field
England

You could also ask children to draw a picture of their living thing, which would be an opportunity to develop the working scientifically skills of observing closely. If clipboards can be provided, this makes it easier for children to do this outside.

In order to address the way in which habitats provide for the basic needs of different kinds of plants and animals, children can write about what they do during the day (as the living thing they have found). They should be encouraged to focus on food and shelter, as well as air, water and space. For example, "I am Sidney the Slug. I eat leaves. I like to live in dark and wet places." Ensure that children wash their hands thoroughly after working outdoors.

Assessment for Learning

Ask children questions such as:
How many legs does the minibeast have?
Do you know the name of it? How can we find out?
Where did you find it? Why do you think that this animal lives in this habitat?

Use children's answers as well as the written work they have produced to explore whether they are able to identify some of the living things they have found and are able to describe how different habitats provide for the basic needs of different kinds of animals and plants.

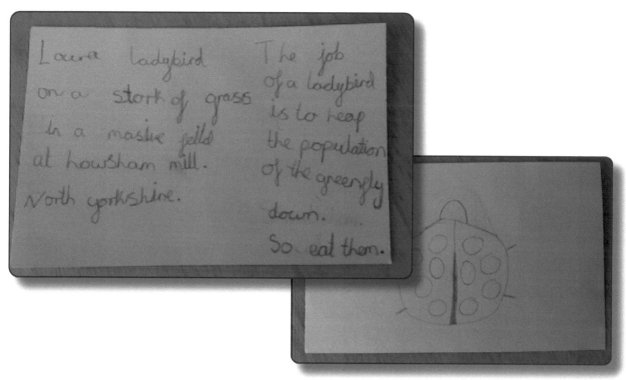

Science Capital

Ask the children to describe their own habitat and how it provides for their needs. If they have pets, or if there are animals at home, can they discuss the habitats of these animals? If the children look after an animal, ask them to discuss what they have to do. Talk about jobs that involve knowledge of animals and plants in their habitats, such as herpetologist, zoologist, environmental scientist and ecologist.

Support

Provide children with a frame to support them in identifying key features of the animal's habitat (see downloads).

⬡ Extension

To add extra challenge for more able children, ask them to carry out further research into the minibeast that they have found and its habitat.

⬡ Follow up

In groups, ask the children to discuss the Concept Cartoon *Worms*. Which of the characters do they agree with and why?

Key vocabulary

Suited, suitable, basic needs, food, shelter, move, feed, names of local habitats, e.g. pond, woodland, etc., names of micro habitats, e.g. under logs, in bushes, etc.

Download resources and links @ www.millgatehouse.co.uk/tpsoresources

6. Plants

Conceptual knowledge

In this activity, children observe and describe how seeds and bulbs grow into mature plants.

Working scientifically

In this activity, children use their observations and ideas to suggest answers to questions.

Assessment

Children meeting the conceptual knowledge objectives will be able to observe seeds and plants growing into mature plants over the course of the academic year. They will be able to describe what they observe.

Children meeting the working scientifically objective will be able to make observations of seeds and bulbs growing into mature plants. They will be able to use these observations to answer questions such as 'What happens if we forget to water the plants?', 'When will there be a flower?', 'When can we eat the beans?'

Activity - Growing healthy plants

Resources needed

Seeds and bulbs – see suggestions below as well as links. (Guidance on plants and bulbs to avoid can be found in *Be Safe!*, section 9, page 19)

Garden trowels suitable for use by children

Watering can, compost

Images or examples of fully-grown vegetables or flowers, so that children can see what the seed or bulb they are planting will grow into

What to do

Children love to sow seeds and plant bulbs. It is usually important to ensure that anything you plant will be ready to harvest during term time. There are many gardeners' calendars available online. A version is provided in the downloadable resources.

Good examples of seeds and bulbs to grow outdoors at school include broad beans, lettuce, onions, peas, potatoes, radishes and tomatoes, as well as daffodils, cornflowers, marigolds, tulips, sweet peas and poppies. If you already have a school garden or allotment, you can use this. If not, choose seeds or bulbs that can be grown in pots outdoors, such as onions or tulips.

Bring in some examples of fully-grown vegetables or pictures of flowers (the ones that you have seeds or bulbs for). Discuss how these plants started life. Show the children the seeds or bulbs and support them in generating questions about what might happen as they grow. This might involve the children working in talking partners or using KWL grids. Ensure that the children's questions are recorded as you will need to refer back to them later in the year.

Follow the instructions on the packet of seeds or bulbs. Make sure that the children all have the opportunity to be involved, This might mean each child planting one seed or bulb – please be aware that not all seeds or bulbs will survive!

Make sure that someone is responsible for watering and weeding – ideally this should be the children.

Take the children outside regularly to observe the growth of their plants. Ask them to record their observations of the plants' growth. This may take the form of photographs, drawings, written descriptions or verbally describing what they observe. There are many opportunities for cross-curricular links here. The children's observations should form the basis for discussion, further generation of questions and the opportunity to discuss the answers to their questions.

Ensure that children wash their hands thoroughly after working outdoors.

Assessment for Learning

Ask the children what has happened to their seeds and bulbs. Prompt them to describe what they can see. Remind them of the questions that they came up with at the start of the year/ topic. Can they use their observations to answer these questions? This might be in written or verbal form.

Science Capital

Find out whether any of the children, or their family members, grow plants at home. Can any of the children tell the rest of the class what seeds or bulbs they have planted at home, when they planted them and how long the plants took to grow? If there is a local area where things are grown, take the children to visit – this might be the school allotment, other local allotments or even a local garden centre. Discuss careers that involve knowledge of plants, such as gardeners, botanists, grocers and chefs.

Support

Children might need to be prompted to observe and describe seeds and bulbs growing into plants. Suitable questions are provided in the downloadable resources.

Extension

To add extra challenge for more able children, they can be more systematic in recording their observations. They may want to cross-reference their findings with other groups or with secondary sources.

Follow up

In groups, ask the children to discuss the Concept Cartoon *Upside down seeds*. Which of the characters do they agree with and why?

Key vocabulary

Leaf, flower, blossom, petal, fruit, berry, root, seed, branch, stem, stalk, bud
Names of garden and wild flowering plants in the local area
Light, shade, Sun, warm, cool, water, grow, healthy

Download resources and links @ www.millgatehouse.co.uk/tpsoresources

7. Animals including humans

Conceptual knowledge

In this activity, children find out about and describe the basic needs of animals, including humans, for survival (water, food and air).

Working scientifically

In this activity, children use observations and ideas to suggest answers to questions.

Assessment

Children meeting the conceptual knowledge objectives will be able to find out about the basic needs of animals by looking for evidence of animals, and link this evidence to what animals need to survive.

Children meeting the working scientifically objective will be able to gather the items and use their observations about the items they have gathered to suggest answers to questions raised.

Activity - Exploring the basic needs of animals

Resources needed

Either a printout of the 'Alien Scavenger Hunt' for each child/pair, or the scavenger hunt displayed centrally somewhere
You may like to provide children with a range of containers to collect their evidence in (paper cups, plastic bags, etc.)
Cameras, tablets or pencil and paper

What to do

Tell the children that they are Zogoids from the planet Zog. Queen Zog has sent them on a mission to Earth to find evidence of humans and other animals. Discuss the fact that they cannot collect humans or other animals, because we (as Zogoids) don't yet know what the animals need to stay alive, to survive.

At this point, it may be appropriate to discuss whether or not humans are animals (humans are animals, but many children are under the misconception that humans are not).

Split the children into groups – each group should be looking for evidence of a different type of animal (including humans). Provide children with cameras, tablets or pencil and paper to record things that cannot be collected, such as birds' nests and footprints.

Discuss the types of evidence that they might find – reiterate that they cannot collect actual animals. Obvious examples might include rubbish, poo, evidence that an animal has eaten something and the homes of animals (habitats). Remind the children that we are hoping to find out what animals need in order to survive. Some children might link this to collecting samples of air and water. You may need to lead other children to this conclusion.

Depending on the site that you are using, you may find evidence such as birds' nests, animal footprints, rubbish or droppings. Further examples can be found in the downloadable table.

You will need to remind the children about the health and safety aspects pertinent to your site. This might include boundaries and what litter they can or can't pick up safely – including poo.

Children could collect the items in the containers provided and use these to provide a prompt for discussion about what they think humans and other animals need to survive.

Ensure that children wash their hands thoroughly after working outdoors.

Assessment for Learning

Children need to present their findings – this could be in the form of a verbal presentation for Queen Zog, a written report or using tablets to photograph and annotate findings.

Use their presentations to explore their understanding about the basic needs of animals for survival and address any misconceptions in subsequent lessons. Ask the children questions about what their evidence suggests that different animals need to survive.

Science Capital

Ask the children about the animals that live in or near their homes; what do these animals need to survive? If any of the children look after pets, or wild birds (for example), ask them to describe how they do this. Discuss careers that involve looking after animals, such as farmers, vets and kennel workers.

Support

Some children may need additional guidance as to the types of things to look for (see Alien Scavenger Hunt 2 in downloads).

Extension

To add extra challenge for more able children, ask them to research what other animals need to survive.

Follow up

Children can write a report for Queen Zog detailing their findings and outlining their conclusions as to what living creatures on Earth need to survive.

> Dear Queen Zog
>
> There are lots of living things on Earth. I have seen foxes and horses. There are birds in the sky and plants on the ground.
>
> *The animals need food and water to live there life. The plants need water and sun to grow. The animals need shelter to cover them.
>
> from charlotte

Key vocabulary

Survive, survival, evidence, habitat, human, water, food, air, nutrition

8. Uses of everyday materials

Conceptual knowledge

In this activity, children identify and compare the suitability of a variety of everyday materials.

Working scientifically

In this activity, children perform simple tests.

Assessment

Children meeting the conceptual knowledge objective will be able to say why they have chosen the materials that they have, for example, "I have chosen leaves and plastic for the roof because it is waterproof; I have not used sticks for the roof, because the gaps let the water in".

Children meeting the working scientifically objective will be able to say how they know which material is 'best' for a purpose. For example, "I know that leaves and plastic are waterproof because I poured water over my pixie house and it stayed dry inside. When I poured water over the pixie house with the roof made of sticks, it got wet inside".

Activity - Exploring materials for a pixie house

Resources needed

In an ideal world, this lesson would take place in a forest area, where there are lots of sticks, leaves and other natural materials around. Additional materials should include different types of cloth (cotton, felt, etc.), plastic carrier bags or cling film, cardboard and paper towel.

What to do

Prepare the materials you want the children to work with.

Discuss what children already know about the materials available to them.

Explain your health and safety rules. These might include the area that the children are allowed to work in and the things they can and cannot pick up.

If possible, put the lesson into a context, such as a story or topic.

Set the task – Can you make a house for a pixie? Discuss what the requirements are for your pixie… Does the pixie need to be warm, dry, protected from predators? You can adapt this depending on the context and the materials available.

Give the children time to explore with the materials available to them and to build a shelter for their pixie.

Children should then carry out simple tests to find out whether the requirements set were met. This is likely to include whether the pixie house is waterproof, warm or windproof.

Ensure that children wash their hands thoroughly after working outdoors.

Assessment for Learning

Discuss with the children how they will know whether the pixie house is waterproof (for example). Ask them how they might find out. Introduce the concept of carrying out a test. Ask questions to encourage the children to be systematic in their testing. What can we add to our design to make it waterproof? Which material worked the best?

Science Capital

Ask the children if they have made dens or shelters in the past. These might include shelters made outdoors as well as pillow forts or cardboard box dens. If there are any local shelters – e.g. woodland areas that contain dens, bus stops, bandstands, etc, discuss what materials these are made from and why. What about rabbit hutches or dog kennels? Discuss the materials that these are made from. Talk about people who might need to know about materials for their jobs, such as a builder, architect or clothes designer.

Support

Children may need to revisit the properties of materials in more detail. Give them the opportunity to explore the properties of the available materials – discuss which materials are soft, hard, bendy, etc. Children may need to be given more guidance/structure in carrying out a test.

Extension

To add extra challenge for more able children, ask them to come up with their own requirements for the 'pixie house' and to come up with tests for these.

Follow up

Children can draw a picture of their shelter or take a photograph of it, and annotate it to explain why they have chosen the materials they have and what tests were carried out.

The plastic tunnel is water proof so the pixie will be dry

The rocks are heavy so the pixie house doesn't blow away

This is a slope to make it easier for the pixies to go into the house

Key vocabulary

Object, material, wood, plastic, water, paper, fabric, card/cardboard, hard, soft, stretchy, stiff, bendy, floppy, waterproof, absorbent, breaks/tears

Download resources and links @ www.millgatehouse.co.uk/tpsoresources

9. Plants

Conceptual knowledge

In this activity, children will explore the requirements of plants for life and growth (light, water, nutrients from soil, and room to grow). NB: Plants also need air – this will need to be addressed separately.

Working scientifically

In this activity, children will set up simple practical enquiries, comparative and fair tests.

Assessment

Children meeting the conceptual knowledge objective will be able to describe how plants need light, water, nutrients from soil and room to grow.

Children meeting the working scientifically objective will be able to set up a test to find out what happens if plants are deprived of light, water, nutrients from soil or room to grow.

Activity - Exploring what plants need to grow

Resources needed

Lots of plants
Tools for planting/potting
Different places in which to grow the plants
One dying plant (or a photograph of a dying plant)

What to do

Show the children a plant that is not looking very healthy. If you do not have one, show them a picture. Ask the children why they think it is dying. Explore their understanding of what a plant needs to grow.

Explain that you have several plants and that you would like the children, in groups, to investigate what the plants need in order to remain alive. Each group should ideally investigate a different variable (light, water, nutrients from the soil and room to grow).

You may wish to use a resource such as 'post it' planning (see downloadable resources and links) to support children in planning their investigations.

Each group should plant two plants (or more if available) in different conditions and keep a record of how well they grow. They should try to ensure that other variables are controlled. In order to meet the working scientifically objective, it is important that the children set up the investigation for themselves. Good practice would also be for the children to do their own planning.

The different conditions that children might change in order to address the curriculum objectives are as follows:
- one plant in the light and one in the dark
- one plant somewhere without water and one with water (plants may need to be under a shelter to prevent the rain disrupting the investigation)
- one plant in soil and one plant in another material such as sand
- one plant in a very tiny pot and one in a large pot.

Ensure that children wash their hands thoroughly after working outdoors.

Assessment for Learning

Children should regularly observe their plants and note their findings. Ask them what their findings are telling them.

Science Capital

Find out which children grow plants at home. Ask whether any family members do any gardening and get the children to share with the class what they have to do to keep their plants alive. Take children to visit places where plants grow. This might include the school field, a local park or garden centre.

Support

Provide the children with step-by-step instructions to support them in planning their investigation.

Extension

To add extra challenge for more able children, they can ask further questions about what a plant needs in order for it to grow. They may wish to investigate whether water could be substituted with fizzy drinks, for example.

Follow up

Children could write a set of instructions about how to look after a plant.

Key vocabulary

Plants, light, warmth, water, leaves, roots, stem, grow, growth, height

Download resources and links @ www.millgatehouse.co.uk/tpsoresources

10. Animals including humans

Conceptual knowledge

In this activity, children will identify that humans have skeletons for support, protection and movement.

Working scientifically

In this activity, children ask relevant questions and use different types of scientific enquiries to answer them.

Assessment

Children meeting the conceptual knowledge objective will be able to identify that humans have skeletons for support, protection and movement.

Children meeting the working scientifically objective will be able to ask relevant questions about skeletons and use different types of scientific enquiries to answer them.

Note: this working scientifically objective will need to be covered in many lessons so that children's questions are addressed using a range of different types of science enquiries.

Activity - Asking questions about skeletons

Resources needed

Whiteboards and pens (or other recording format)
Tape measures
PE equipment

What to do

This lesson should take place after children have had the opportunity to learn about the names of different bones in the human body.

Ask the children to create a land-art model of a skeleton using resources such as sticks and leaves found in the outdoor setting. Use this to address any misconceptions about skeletons.

Discuss what would happen if we did not have skeletons. Encourage the children to consider whether we would be able to stand up, how our organs would be protected and how we might move.

Ask the children to discuss what differences there might be between one person's skeleton and another. This might include longer legs, larger skulls and bigger arm-spans. Care should be taken around any sensitivities that may be linked to this in your cohort.

Encourage the children to work in groups to generate their own questions about the skeletons of their classmates. These questions might include, 'Can children with longer legs jump further?', 'Can taller children run faster?' or 'Can children with bigger hands throw further?' You will need to ensure that the questions the children are generating can be investigated with the available cohort – it may be possible to 'borrow' some older or younger children to answer some of the questions.

Support the children in planning their pattern-seeking investigations and record the results. This might be on whiteboards, in books or on tablets.

Ensure that children wash their hands thoroughly after working outdoors.

Assessment for Learning

The initial land-art skeleton provides a good opportunity for Assessment for Learning, giving you the opportunity to identify children's initial misconceptions.

The conversation that you have with children as part of the lesson also provides a chance to carry out Assessment for Learning - see the suggested discussion points earlier.

Children should be given the opportunity to articulate what question they were investigating, how they carried out their investigation and what their findings were. This provides an excellent opportunity for you to explore whether children understand what their skeleton is for, and whether they have been able to ask relevant questions and identify which type of enquiry they have been doing. Planning for future lessons can be adapted accordingly.

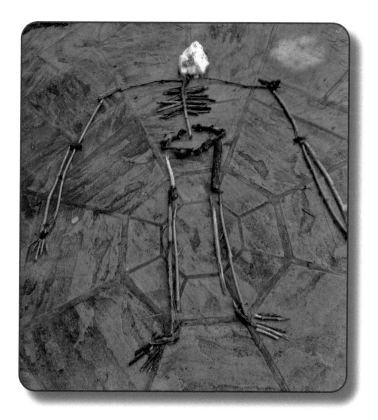

Science Capital

Find out if any of the children have broken bones in the past – they may have x-ray images that they can share; they may know the names of particular bones. Discuss how the foods that we eat and the exercise that we do helps to strengthen our bones and muscles. Explore careers linked to sports and radiology.

Support

Provide children with a frame on which to record results (see downloads).

Extension

To add extra challenge for more able children, encourage them to try to use more than one enquiry type to investigate the answers to their questions; for example, they might carry out some research to try and find answers.

Follow up

Children could discuss the question, 'What if I didn't have bones?' They could then write about what it would be like if they didn't have bones, drawing on their understanding of the role that the skeleton plays in support, protection and movement.

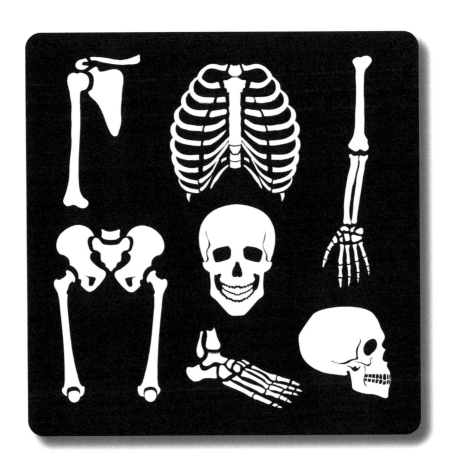

Key vocabulary

Skeleton, bones, muscles, joints, support, protect, move, skull, ribs, spine, function

11. Rocks

⬡ Conceptual knowledge

In this activity, children will recognise that soils are made from rocks and organic matter.

⬡ Working scientifically

In this activity, children make systematic and careful observations.

⬡ Assessment

Children meeting the conceptual knowledge objectives will be able to describe what different soil samples are made up of. This may be verbally, or through their written observations.

Children meeting the working scientifically objective will be able to observe different soil samples and describe the similarities and differences between them.

Activity - Investigating what soils are made from

Resources needed

Several types of soil – these might include soil from the school field, soil from near a river, compost or soil from a range of different children's gardens. Make sure that samples are taken from safe areas, e.g. no broken glass, not contaminated by dog or cat fouling. Ideally, take a photo from where each sample came from.
Large sheets of paper and felt tip pens/chalk for writing on playground
Large clear containers (large old mayonnaise jars would be good), or graduated cylinders
Magnifying glasses
Old cutlery or lollipop sticks

What to do

If possible, take the children to different locations to dig up a number of different types of soil. If this is not possible, have soil samples ready prepared – ideally take a photograph of where each sample came from.

Take each sample of soil and put it on a large sheet of paper – or on the playground. The children then examine each sample using magnifying glasses. They should be given the opportunity to touch the soil samples and describe the texture, and use any tools (lollipop sticks/old cutlery etc.) to explore the soil samples. Support the children in writing their observations on large sheets of paper, or in chalk on the playground. Give them the opportunity to make observations of all the soil types to discuss the similarities and differences between them. You may wish to introduce them to the terms 'organic' and 'inorganic'.

The children then take a sample of each type of soil and put it in a clear container. This should be topped up with water and children then make observations over the next day or so. Organic material will float to the top, so they will be able to see that some soils contain a greater quantity of organic material than others.

Ensure that children wash their hands thoroughly after working outdoors.

Assessment for Learning

Children should make observations of both the soil samples and the samples in jars. Ask them to write down or discuss their observations.

Find out whether the children can use appropriate vocabulary to describe their soil samples and identify similarities and differences between them.

Science Capital

Talk to the children about the soils that they may be familiar with – this might include soil in the garden, areas of the school field or the soil near a local riverbank. Discuss different STEM professionals who need to know about soil types – these might include a gardener, a geologist or a construction engineer.

Support

Give the children a vocabulary list to support them in making their observations (see downloads).

Extension

To challenge more able children, ask them to raise their own questions about different soil types and plan investigations to find out the answers. These might include which soil is the best for growing beans in, which soil absorbs the most water and which soil is best for building on.

Follow up

Ask the children to summarise their findings by writing a short report about the different soil types.

Key vocabulary

Rock, stone, pebble, boulder, grain, crystals, layers, hard, soft, texture, absorb water, soil, fossil, marble, chalk, granite, sandstone, slate, soil, peat, sandy/chalk/clay soil, organic, inorganic, difference, similarity

12. Light

Conceptual knowledge

In this activity, children recognise that shadows are formed when the light from a light source is blocked by an opaque object.

Working scientifically

In this activity, children record findings using drawings and labelled diagrams.

Assessment

Children meeting the conceptual knowledge objective will be able to explain that their shadows are formed when an opaque object blocks the light from the Sun.

Children meeting the working scientifically objective will be able to draw a picture that shows a light source, an object and a shadow in the correct places.

Activity - Exploring shadows

Resources needed

Large cotton sheet(s) or huge sheets of paper (the back of wallpaper for example)
Opaque objects (these could be natural materials such as pine cones or twigs)
Pencil and paper, clipboards (alternatively tablets on which children can annotate photographs)

What to do

This lesson needs to take place on a sunny day in an area with direct sunlight! It's a great way of introducing children to the concept of shadows and finding out what they already know.

Ideally this lesson would take place in an area where there are lots of sticks, leaves and other natural materials around – requiring little preparation. Give the children sheets of material (old bed sheets) or large pieces of paper on which to create shadows. Provide them with a range of opaque objects. Avoid using transparent or translucent materials in the first lesson, but later repeat the lesson with these materials included. Avoid using mirrors or other reflective materials, as this can lead to misconceptions this early in the topic.

Explain your health and safety rules. These might include the area that the children are allowed to work in, and the things they can and cannot pick up.

Set the task – Can you create some shadow art? Can you work in pairs to decorate your partner's shadow?

Give the children time to explore with the materials available to them.

Whilst the children are exploring shadows, take photographs – or ask the children to take their own photographs of their shadows.

It is also a good idea to repeat this lesson indoors with torches (avoid high-intensity LED torches), so that the children experience a variety of different light sources.

Find out if children know what the term 'opaque' means. Repeat the lesson on another sunny day using transparent, translucent and opaque materials.

Give children the opportunity to draw a picture of what they have been doing and label the light source, object and shadow.

Ensure that children wash their hands thoroughly after working outdoors.

Assessment for Learning

At the start of the lesson, discuss what the children already know about shadows. Do they think that they could lose their shadow? Ask the children how shadows are made. Can they explain that shadows are made when an object blocks the light source (the sunlight)?

Science Capital

Ask the children about any shadow shapes that they might make at home. Have they made shadow puppets? Talk about any local areas such as woodlands or bridges where shadows are cast, and children are in shade. Are there any families with artistic interests who may have created shadow art?

Support

Ask the children to annotate their photograph before drawing their own picture, so that they are more secure in their understanding when they come to creating their own labelled diagram.

Extension

To add extra challenge for more able children, ask them to repeat the task but with the light source in a different place. What happens to the shadow?

Follow up

In groups, ask the children to discuss the Concept Cartoon *Two trees*. Which of the characters do they agree with and why?

Key vocabulary

Light, light source, dark, absence of light, transparent, translucent, opaque, shiny, matt, surface, shadow, reflect, mirror, sunlight, dangerous

13. Forces and magnets

Conceptual knowledge

In this activity, children will compare how things move on different surfaces.

Working scientifically

In this activity, children use results to draw simple conclusions.

Assessment

Children meeting the conceptual knowledge objectives will be able to describe which surface is easiest to move the sledge over.

Children meeting the working scientifically objective will be able to write (or say) a conclusion based on their results. This conclusion should state which surface it is easiest to move the sledge over.

Activity - Exploring friction with sledges

Resources needed

One 'sledge' for each group of children – this needs to have a rope or string attached to pull it along. A cardboard box from a supermarket would suffice. Please be aware, if using a real sledge, that the bottom may get scratched.
Something reasonably heavy to put in the sledge (if safe to do so, use a child!)

What to do

This activity would be amazing if done on a snowy day – but not essential!

Find out what the children already know about friction by discussing their experience of sledging. If they are not familiar with the concept, it may be helpful to share a video clip of sledging before the lesson.

The term 'friction' should be introduced to the children. Friction is a force between two surfaces that are sliding, or trying to slide, across each other. Ask the children to rub their hands together quickly - the heat produced is caused by friction.

Give each group of children a sledge with a weight in it (this weight may be a child – please risk assess for your circumstances). Although this investigation will not be a 'fair test', it is important to reinforce the concept of trying to keep variables the same – that is, the weight should be kept the same. The children should be given time to try pulling the sledge with the weight across a variety of different surfaces. Ask them to make predictions about which surfaces will be the easiest to pull the sledge across and which will be the most difficult.

The children then record their results on a whiteboard or clipboard.

Ensure that children wash their hands thoroughly after working outdoors.

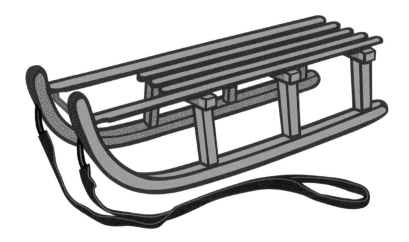

Assessment for Learning

Ask the children to write a conclusion based on their results. Which surface was it easier to pull the sledge over? Which surface was the most difficult? What does this tell us about the amount of friction between the two surfaces? You may want the children to verbally record their conclusion rather than write it down.

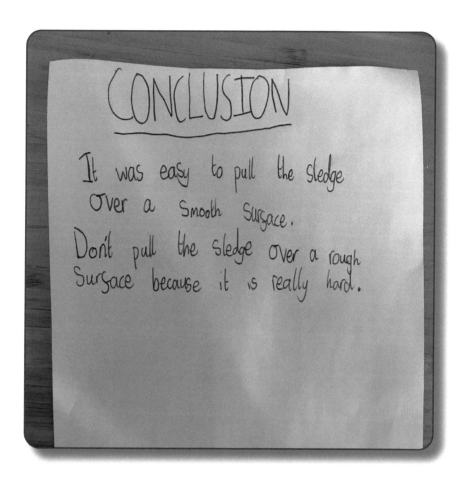

Science Capital

Talk to the children about their experience using sledges – which surfaces make the sledge go faster and which slow it down? Discuss examples of friction (or lack of friction) that they may have experience of, such as ice skating, using a slide and different types of shoes for different purposes. Talk about examples of useful friction such as when braking on a bike. Mention how designers and engineers need to consider friction when creating products such as shoes and vehicles.

Support

Give children a frame in which to write their results (see downloads).

Extension

To add extra challenge for more able pupils, ask them to apply their knowledge by choosing which surface will be best for a spinner to spin on.

Follow up

Ask the children to design a poster that draws attention to the dangers of an icy playground.

Key vocabulary

Force, push, pull, twist, contact force, non-contact force, friction

Download resources and links @ www.millgatehouse.co.uk/tpsoresources

14. Living things and their habitats

⬡ Conceptual knowledge

In this activity, children recognise that living things can be grouped in a variety of ways.

⬡ Working scientifically

In this activity, children record findings using simple scientific language, drawings and tables.

⬡ Assessment

Children meeting the conceptual knowledge objective will be able to suggest different ways of grouping a set of living things (such as plants). This might include by colour, size or shape. To judge whether or not the children are able to do this, ask them to sort items they have found into groups. This will need to be repeated in order to demonstrate that living things can be grouped in a variety of ways.

Children meeting the working scientifically objective will be able to use simple scientific language to explain how they have grouped living things. They will be able to draw pictures that show the differences between things in each group, and they will be able to use a table to group objects.

Activity - Grouping things in different ways

Resources needed

Hoops (PE) or chalk to mark out hoops
Rope or chalk to mark out lines

What to do

Start by asking the children to work in groups to collect items that can be found in your outdoor setting. This could include leaves, sticks, plants, flowers, shells, fir cones, etc. Depending on your context and setting, you may need to warn children against picking up rubbish, etc.

Challenge the children to come up with as many different ways of grouping items as possible. This might include by colour, size and shape. This will help them to develop their understanding of how to classify items.

Ask children and adults to question the way in which items are grouped. There may be issues such as some children having overly specific groups, such as 'spiky leaf with 10 black marks' and 'crinkly big leaf', or items that belong in multiple categories such as 'big' and 'green'.

Model different ways of grouping items using the two hoops (or equivalent). Ensure that the children know what a table, Venn diagram and Carroll diagram are. Encourage them to use their scientific understanding and vocabulary to group living things.

Children should record their groupings in tables and drawings. This might be by using natural materials, or by writing on a whiteboard, or using a clipboard.

A child might be able to sort leaves into groups such as green/red/yellow, spiky/not spiky. They could present this outdoors by simply piling leaves up initially, and then by drawing a Carroll diagram (or similar) with a stick and sorting their leaves in a variety of ways.

Once the children are confident with grouping living things – this might be during a second lesson – support them in searching for minibeasts, drawing pictures of them and grouping them in a number of different ways, such as wings/no wings, 8 legs/6 legs/no legs, slimy/not slimy. Children could present this as a table – or simply by drawing groups of minibeasts.

Ensure that children wash their hands thoroughly after working outdoors.

Assessment for Learning

Now ask the children to collect something different and group the items. This may need to be repeated a number of times before the children are secure with the concept of grouping and classifying.

Ask the children why they have grouped the living things as they have, and whether there are any alternative ways of grouping the living things.

Science Capital

Talk about occasions at home when the children may have to sort and classify objects – my toys go in the red box; my brother's toys go in the yellow box, for example. Be explicit about how this skill is used by STEM professionals such as zoologists, ecologists and palaeontologists.

Support

Give the children a frame (such as two hula hoops) in which to sort their items. A written frame is available for this (see downloads).

Extension

To add extra challenge for more able children, ask them to choose how best to present their findings. Some children may be able to start producing classification keys.

Follow up

Repeating this activity with a range of different living things either indoors or outdoors will ensure that children have a good understanding of how to group living things. There are many opportunities for cross-curricular maths work here too.

Key vocabulary

Classification, classification keys, environment, habitat, organism, minibeast

15. Animals including humans

Conceptual knowledge

In this activity, children identify producers, predators and prey in food chains.

Working scientifically

In this activity, children ask relevant questions about food chains.

Assessment

Children meeting the conceptual knowledge objective will be able to name the animals and plants in the food chain modelled and state whether they are producers, predators or prey.

Children meeting the working scientifically objective will be able to ask relevant questions such as 'What would happen to the caterpillars if there were no blue tits?'

Activity - Interpreting food chains

Resources needed

Food chain cards - see downloads
Tag rugby tags
Bean bags
Coloured bibs (used for team sports)
Hula hoops or other containers are also useful
PE whistle

What to do

Use the food chain cards (see downloads) to discuss food chains with the children. They should have been introduced to food chains, but may not have encountered the terms 'producer', 'predator' and 'prey' previously. Use these terms when allocating roles to the children.

Divide the children into groups. The majority will be 'caterpillars' and should be given bibs of a particular colour. About a third of the children will be 'blue tits' and should be given bibs of a different colour. One or two children should be 'sparrow hawks' and should be given yet another different-coloured bib. All of the children except for the 'sparrow hawks' will need a tag rugby tag. The bean bags represent the leaves.

The bean bags should be put in one place – at the end of a football field for example (the children start at the other end). The 'caterpillars' will need to 'eat' at least 5 bean bags (leaves) in order to survive. They can only collect one bean bag at a time and must return their bean bag back to the starting point. If each 'caterpillar' has a hula hoop or other container in which to place their 'leaves', this is helpful. 'Caterpillars' should be given a few seconds' head start. At this point, 'blue tits' are released. 'Blue tits' need to eat at least two 'caterpillars' in order to survive. They do this by taking a tag rugby tag. 'Blue tits' should be given a few seconds' head start before 'sparrow hawks' are released. 'Sparrow hawks' need to eat at least two 'blue tits' in order to survive. Depending on the speed and number of children, you may need to adapt these quantities.

After a few children have been caught, blow the whistle and stop the game. Discuss who has eaten enough food. Play several rounds varying quantities of food. Encourage the children to ask questions about the food chain.

Ensure that children wash their hands thoroughly after working outdoors.

Assessment for Learning

Use the food chain cards to explore the children's prior knowledge of food chains. Ask the children to suggest other food chains that they may be familiar with. Use this information to revisit the age 6-7 objective if necessary. Ask children if they can describe the role of different animals and plants in the food chain, eliciting the scientific vocabulary of predator, prey and consumer. What questions do they have about food chains?

Science Capital

Discuss the children's experience of food chains. This may include feeding pets or wild birds. If the children are from a farming background, they may be able to talk more knowledgeably about what animals eat and which animals humans eat. If possible, take children on a local visit where they can explore food chains further. This might include to a farm, a nature reserve or park, where they can see birds eating seeds or worms, or even a bug hunt in the school grounds. Consider engaging with 'Farmertime' if children have limited experience of farms or the countryside.

Support

Provide the children with question starters (see downloads).

⬡ Extension

To add extra challenge for more able children, challenge them to come up with their own food chain game.

⬡ Follow up

In groups, ask the children to discuss the Concept Cartoon *Rabbits and foxes*. Which of the characters do they agree with and why?

Key vocabulary

Producer, predator, prey, food chain

Download resources and links @ www.millgatehouse.co.uk/tpsoresources

16. States of matter

Conceptual knowledge

In this activity, children observe that some materials change state when they are heated or cooled.

Working scientifically

In this activity, children identify changes related to the process of heating or cooling.

Assessment

Children meeting the conceptual knowledge objective will be able to state that **some** materials change state when heated over an open fire, making statements such as 'chocolate changes from a solid to a liquid when heated'.

Children meeting the working scientifically objective will be able to outline the properties of items that are solids, liquids and gases and describe how these have changed during the process of heating or cooling, for example; 'the liquid chocolate is runny and can be poured. When it is cooled, it becomes a solid and cannot be poured'.

Activity - Heating and cooling materials

Resources needed

An open fire or camp stove. Use a proper camp stove with care – do NOT be tempted to use a spirit (methylated spirit, alcohol) burner.
Access to water
Fire gloves or tongs
Handwashing facilities
Depending on the activity chosen, you will need some of these resources:
Ice, bananas, tin foil, chocolate, pan, rice crispies, cake cases, instant hot chocolate powder

What to do

Different local authorities, academy chains and senior leadership teams have different policies regarding cooking on an open fire. Make sure you follow appropriate guidance, risk assess accordingly and spend time discussing your health and safety rules with the children. Fires should only be lit and supervised by members of staff who are experienced and confident around fires. If necessary, attend appropriate training.

Discuss with the children what they already know about solids, liquids and gases. Challenge them to find a solid, a liquid and a gas in the environment. There may be puddles nearby – if not, strategically bring a bottle of water with you. If there is evidence of significant prior knowledge, ask the children to represent their understanding of solids, liquids and gases using natural materials as an Assessment for Learning activity. Alternatively, this could be done at the end of the lesson.

Try one or two of the following:

Boil some water in a pan over the fire. Watch the water as it evaporates from the pan. Discuss what change has occurred. The water could then be used to make instant hot chocolate. Heat some ice to melt it into water, and then watch it evaporate.

Cut bananas open (leave the skins on) and put chocolate buttons or squares of chocolate inside. Wrap in tin foil and heat on the embers of the fire. After a few minutes, lift off the fire (using fire gloves or tongs) and eat the melted gooey chocolatey banana…

Break some chocolate and put it in a pan over the fire or stove. Help the children to stir the chocolate until it melts. Mix the melted chocolate with some rice crispies and make rice crispie cakes. If it is a cold day, these will solidify quite quickly. On a warmer day, you may need to refrigerate them.

If you are going to eat things, ensure scrupulous attention to hygiene, e.g. thorough hand-washing. See *Be Safe!* section 7, page 15.

Assessment for Learning

Ask the children to represent their understanding of solids, liquids and gases using natural or found materials.

Throughout this lesson, ask children to describe the changes that they observe. Questions might include: What has happened to the chocolate? Why has it melted?

Science Capital

Talk to the children about their experiences with melting things – this might include cooking on a fire or melting ice lollies. Ask them about when they have observed evaporation – have they seen a puddle that has dried up? Have any of the children been ice skating? Is there an ice rink or a metal furnace nearby? Chemistry researchers, chefs, metal fabricators and nutritionists might need to know about changing state. You might also want to make links to working as a firefighter.

Support

Give children a solid, such as an ice cube or a chocolate button, that they can melt in their hands.

Extension

To add extra challenge for more able children, ask them to think of (or find) items that do not change state when they are heated or cooled. Is this because we cannot heat them to a high enough temperature (metal for example) or is this because these items do not melt (wood burns rather than melts)?

Follow up

Back in the classroom, you could ask children to write or draw what happened. They could also annotate an image to demonstrate their understanding.

Key vocabulary

Solid, liquid, gas, state change, melting, freezing, melting point, boiling point, evaporation, temperature

17. Sound

Conceptual knowledge

In this activity, children recognise that sounds get fainter as the distance from the sound source increases.

Working scientifically

In this activity, children take accurate measurements using data loggers.

Assessment

Children meeting the conceptual knowledge objective will be able recognise that sounds get fainter as the distance from the sound source increases.

Children meeting the working scientifically objective will be able to use a data logger to take measurements of a sound.

Activity - Using a datalogger to measure sound

Resources needed

A trumpet or other loud instrument and someone who can play it
Trundle wheel (to measure metres)
Data loggers
Pen and paper/tablet on which to record findings

What to do

Prior to this lesson, you may need to teach the children how to use your data loggers depending on their familiarity with them.

Ask a child to play the trumpet outdoors in the school field or in a local park.

The other children use data loggers to measure the noise level at different distances from the source of the sound. Depending on the type of data loggers being used, children may be able to save their results on the data logger, perhaps doing a snapshot every ten metres, or they may need to note their findings as they go. Clearly background noise will be a factor and you will need to adapt this activity to suit your context.

It can be helpful to measure the volume in a range of different directions from the source of the sound to ensure that the children don't think that sound only travels in one direction.

Ensure that children wash their hands thoroughly after working outdoors.

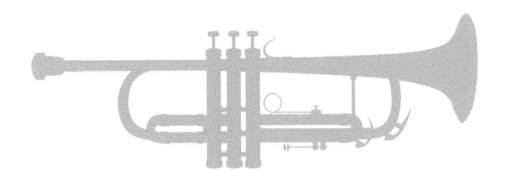

Assessment for Learning

Ask the children what they think happens to the volume of sounds as they move further away from the source of the sound. Get them to explain why they think that sounds are fainter the further away from the source you get.

Science Capital

Talk about noises that the children can hear from their homes or the school. The focus should be on noises that they will know are louder when they are nearby, such as trains, roads or farmyards, rather than things that they may not have experienced close up, such as an aeroplane. Talk to the children about STEM professionals who might need to know about the volume of sounds at different distances, such as musicians and sound engineers. Many children will have experienced going to the pantomime, so this might be an appropriate example to discuss.

Support

Provide children with a frame in which to record their findings (see downloads).

Extension

To add extra challenge for more able children, ask them to record their findings in a line graph.

Follow up

Children could write a letter to the neighbours of the school asking whether they can hold an outdoor performance in the school grounds. They could outline what the expected level of noise would be if the school neighbours were to come to the performance versus staying at home.

Key vocabulary

Sound, source, vibrate, vibration, travel, volume, faint, loud, insulation

18. Electricity

Conceptual knowledge

In this activity, children recognise some common conductors and insulators, and associate metals with being good conductors.

Working scientifically

In this activity, children set up simple comparative tests.

Assessment

Children meeting the conceptual knowledge objective will be able to state which materials are conductors and which are insulators. They will be able to describe how metals are conductors of electricity.

Children meeting the working scientifically objective will be able to set up a simple comparative test to find out which materials are conductors and which are insulators.

Activity - Recognising conductors and insulators

Resources needed

Per group:

3 wires

1 bulb

1 battery (Do not use batteries that can give high discharge currents, such as rechargeable batteries. Zinc-carbon are safer)

Depending on the types of equipment you have, you may also need a bulb holder, battery holder and crocodile clips

Depending on what there is in your outdoor setting, you may need to provide children with a range of objects to test. These could include a lolly stick, a spoon, a pen, a tennis racquet and a baton

Pen and paper/whiteboard/tablet on which to record results

What to do

This lesson should take place once the children have had the opportunity to learn about simple circuits. Each group should be given the resources to make a simple circuit and should test items that they find in the environment, or are provided with, to see whether they are conductors or insulators.

Ask the children to set up their own simple tests – you may want to bring out a range of additional unnecessary equipment to enable them to choose their equipment for themselves.

Children could be asked to come up with their own approach to recording their findings or could be provided with a frame.

Ensure that children wash their hands thoroughly after working outdoors.

Assessment for Learning

Ask the children what they already know about conductors and insulators. If they already understand that metal is a conductor, ask them to test a range of different types of metals to find out whether there is a difference in conductivity between different metals.

Science Capital

Discuss the children's experiences of using electrical products. What are they made of? Why might that be? Elicit understanding that electrical products are usually made of insulative material. Discuss jobs that involve knowledge of electricity, conductors and insulators, such as electricians and architects.

Support

Give children a frame in which to record their results (see downloads).

Extension

To add extra challenge for more able children, ask them to test a wider range of materials including different types of metals.

Follow up

Ask the children to apply their knowledge by making a circuit board quiz. They will need to ensure that parts of the board are made of insulative material and that only the wires are conductors.

Key vocabulary

Electricity, electrical appliance/device, electrical circuit, complete circuit, component, cell, battery, positive, negative, connect/connections, loose connection, crocodile clip, bulb, conductor, insulator, metal, non-metal

Download resources and links @ www.millgatehouse.co.uk/tpsoresources

19. Living things and their habitats

⬡ Conceptual knowledge

In this activity, children describe the life process of reproduction in some plants.

⬡ Working scientifically

In this activity, children plan scientific enquiries in order to answer questions about plant reproduction.

⬡ Assessment

Children meeting the conceptual knowledge objective will be able to explain how some plants reproduce asexually and some reproduce sexually.

Children meeting the working scientifically objective will be able to plan an investigation into plants which reproduce asexually.

Activity - Finding out about asexual reproduction

Resources needed

Examples of plants that reproduce asexually: moss, ferns, bulbs, tubers (eg. potatoes) and runners (eg. spider plants or strawberries). Images are available (see downloads)

Compost (ideally a potting compost), scissors, rosemary or thyme plants, plant pots, African violet plants, dandelion plants, labels, garden trowels or old spoons

What to do

This lesson should ideally follow a lesson that involves dissecting a flower to revise the parts of a plant and their role in sexual reproduction.

Start by asking the children how plants reproduce. They should be able to describe the life cycle of flowering plants, including pollination, seed formation and seed dispersal.

Ask the children whether there are any other ways in which plants can reproduce. They may have experienced potatoes and onions sprouting in the cupboard, or they may have experience of taking cuttings.

Show the children examples of plants that reproduce asexually – these include moss, ferns, bulbs, tubers and runners. If you are able to, use real life examples – otherwise, use photographs (see downloads). Ask them to discuss how they think these plants reproduce. Explain that some plants reproduce asexually as well as sexually. Although this happens naturally with many plants, gardeners often force asexual reproduction by taking cuttings.

Give the children a number of plants and ask them to plan an investigation into asexual reproduction. You may find it helpful to give them access to the planning proformas to support this (see downloads).

The children then plan an investigation that involves taking root cuttings, leaf cuttings and stem cuttings from all three plants. They plant these cuttings and make observations over a period of time.

Rosemary and thyme plants should reproduce from stem cuttings. African violets should reproduce from leaf cuttings. Dandelions should reproduce from root cuttings. African violets will need to be kept indoors, but the others can be grown outdoors.

Further information and guidance about growing plants from cuttings can be found on the Royal Horticultural Society website (see links).

Ensure that children wash their hands thoroughly after working outdoors.

Assessment for Learning

Find out what the children already know about plant reproduction and address misconceptions. Ask them how they will find out how the different plants reproduce asexually. Ask children what they think will happen – which plants will be able to reproduce asexually?

Science Capital

Discuss the children's experiences of taking cuttings at home. Ask them whether they have seen potatoes or onions sprouting in the cupboard at home. Find out whether children or their family members are keen gardeners. Discuss careers that involve knowledge of asexual plant reproduction, including gardener, botanist and ecologist.

Support

Provide the children with a frame on which to plan their investigation (see downloads).

Extension

To add extra challenge for more able children, give them a wider range of plants from which to take cuttings.

Follow up

Ask children to carry out research into the different ways in which plants reproduce, and to write a report summarising their findings.

Key vocabulary

Life cycle, reproduce, sexual, fertilises, asexual, plantlets, runners, bulbs, cuttings, flower, seed, clone, propagation, runners

20. Animals including humans

◆ Conceptual knowledge

In this activity, children compare the gestation periods of other animals with humans.

◆ Working scientifically

In this activity, children represent data using scatter graphs and bar graphs.

◆ Assessment

Children meeting the conceptual knowledge objective will be able to use their bar graphs and scatter graphs to identify similarities and differences in the gestation periods of different mammals.

Children meeting the working scientifically objective will be able to represent data using scatter graphs and bar graphs.

Key facts cards	
The gestation period of a cat is 62 days	The gestation period of a horse is 336 days
The gestation period of a dog is 62 days	The gestation period of a human is 275 days
The gestation period of an elephant is 624 days	The gestation period of a pig is 115 days
The gestation period of a hippopotamus is 62 days	The gestation period of a rabbit is 31 days

Activity - Researching gestation periods

⬡ Resources needed

Chalk, if marking on a playground
Objects to mark out axes, such as ropes or long sticks if working on grass

⬡ What to do

Children could research the gestation periods of animals outdoors by following a trail of key fact cards (see downloads) in the school grounds. Alternatively, children could take books or tablets outdoors for carrying out research, or the research could be done indoors prior to the lesson.

Children should also have already had input on bar charts and/or scatter graphs in their maths lessons.

Ask the children to represent their data about gestation periods on a bar chart using chalk or materials such as sticks and rope. Then represent their data about the weights of different newborn animals alongside gestation periods on a scatter graph.

Children should identify patterns in the data. This is likely to include noticing that smaller animals tend to have shorter gestation periods or that animals with shorter life spans tend to have shorter gestation periods.

Ensure that children wash their hands thoroughly after working outdoors.

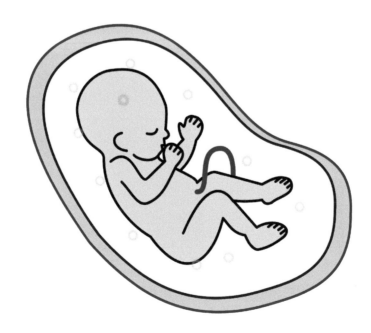

Assessment for Learning

Ask the children to describe the key features of a bar chart or scatter graph. Once the bar charts and scatter graphs are completed, ask questions about what the graphs tell them about the gestation periods of other animals compared to the gestation period of a human.

Science Capital

Children may know about the gestation period of humans because they have younger siblings and have been aware of their mother's pregnancy. They may also have knowledge of the gestation period of animals that they have had as pets. Draw on this knowledge to further discussion. Discuss jobs in which professionals may need to know about gestation periods, such as being a farmer, vet, midwife or conservation worker.

Support

Children could be given a bar chart frame into which to add their data.

Extension

To add extra challenge for more able children, allow them to choose they way in which they present their data.

Follow up

Children could undertake further research into expected life span and gestation period, creating additional scatter graphs.

Key vocabulary

Development, gestation, mass, weight, mammal, offspring, young

21. Properties of and changes in materials

Conceptual knowledge

In this activity, children demonstrate that changes of state are reversible changes and explain that some changes result in the formation of new materials, and that this kind of change is not usually reversible, including changes associated with burning.

Working scientifically

In this activity, children report and present findings from enquiries, including causal relationships, in oral or written forms such as displays and other presentations.

Assessment

Children meeting the conceptual knowledge objective will be able to say which changes are reversible and which are irreversible, for example, burning a marshmallow or cooking dough is an irreversible change; melting chocolate is a reversible change.

Children meeting the working scientifically objective will be able to report and present their findings. This could be in written form, in the form of a PowerPoint presentation, or by orally presenting findings back to their peers or through an assembly.

Activity - Exploring reversible change

Resources needed

An open fire or camp stove. Do not be tempted to use a spirit burner (methylated spirit, alcohol), use a proper camping stove
Access to water, fire gloves or tongs, facilities to clean hands
Depending on the activities chosen, you will need some of these resources: chocolate digestives, marshmallows, sticks for cooking marshmallows, wood to burn, egg(s), orange(s)

What to do

Make sure you follow your local authority, academy chain or Senior Leadership Team's policy on cooking on an open fire and risk assess accordingly. Fires should only be lit and supervised by members of staff who are experienced and confident around fires. If necessary, attend appropriate training.

Discuss what the children already know about changing state. Challenge them to find a solid, a liquid and a gas in the environment and represent their understanding of each using natural materials.

Ask the children what will happen to a piece of wood if it is put on the fire. They may suggest that it will change state (melt). If they have experience of fires (through Cubs, Brownies or using a wood burner at home, etc.), they may know that it will eventually turn to ash and smoke. Put the wood on the fire and observe changes regularly. When wood is burnt, you get ash and smoke. This is a chemical reaction because new substances are formed.

Get the children to cook marshmallows on a stick over the fire. Soak wooden sticks in water to reduce the chance of them catching fire - or use 'green sticks', freshly cut from trees. Put a hot marshmallow between two chocolate biscuits to make s'mores. Discuss the changes that have happened to the chocolate on the biscuit and the marshmallow. The melting chocolate shows a reversible change; the melted/burnt marshmallow shows an irreversible change. Ask the children whether they could reverse the change to the marshmallow. If they believe that it is possible, give them the chance to explore these ideas.

Cooking an egg in an orange is another example of irreversible change. Scoop out the flesh of the orange and crack an egg into the hollowed out skin and heat over the embers.

Children can report their findings by working in groups and presenting their findings back to each other in the outdoor setting, or in the form of a PowerPoint presentation that could be presented to parents or shared with another class.

If you are going to eat things, ensure scrupulous attention to hygiene, e.g. thorough hand-washing. See Be Safe! section 7, page 15.

Assessment for Learning

Discuss with the children what they already know about changing state, which they will have covered previously, then challenge them to find a solid, a liquid and a gas in the environment. Ask the children to represent their understanding of solids, liquids and gases using natural materials as an Assessment for Learning activity.

Throughout this lesson, encourage the children to describe the changes that they observe, ensuring that vocabulary such as change of state, reversible/non-reversible/irreversible change, burning and new material is introduced or revisited.

Science Capital

Discuss the children's experiences of cooking on a fire, or of using a fire to keep warm. Is there a local place where a bonfire night or other event that involves a fire takes place? Link children's experiences to the science of changing state. Does anyone who lives with the children work as a chef or cook? Discuss the science of changing state that is used in their jobs.

Support

Provide a frame to support children in reporting their findings (see downloads).

Extension

To add extra challenge for more able children, ask them to think of further examples of reversible and irreversible change.

Follow up

Challenge children to create a game that other children could play. This game should include many examples of reversible and irreversible changes.

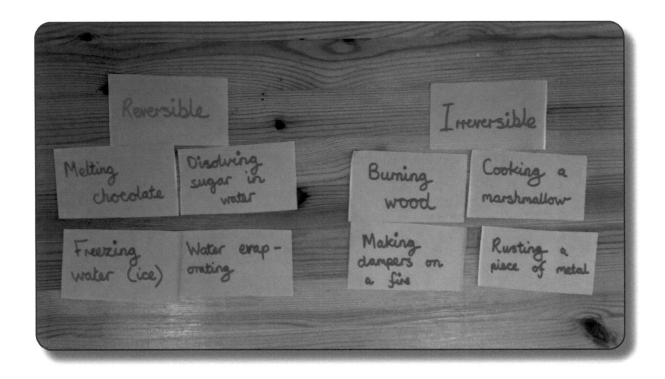

Key vocabulary

Change of state, reversible/non-reversible/irreversible change, burning, new material, melting, solidify, solidifying

22. Earth and space

⬡ Conceptual knowledge

In this activity, children describe the movement of the Earth and other planets relative to the Sun in the solar system.

⬡ Working scientifically

In this activity, children identify scientific evidence that has been used to support or refute ideas or arguments.

⬡ Assessment

Children meeting the conceptual knowledge objective will be able to describe the order of the planets and create an approximate scale model of the solar system.

Children meeting the working scientifically objective will be able to describe how ideas about the solar system have developed, understanding how the geocentric model of the solar system gave way to the heliocentric model.

Activity - Modelling the solar system

Resources needed

Plasticine or clay
Trundle wheel
Signs to mark out the planets
Camera or tablet

What to do

This lesson should take place after researching the work of scientists such as Ptolemy, Alhazen and Copernicus. The children should have an understanding of how the geocentric model of the solar system gave way to the heliocentric model. This lesson will support their understanding of the heliocentric model.

First, the children carry out research into the planets in the solar system, in particular the sizes of the planets and their distances from the Sun. Good websites for research include:

- The National Schools' Observatory
- Spacekids
- NASA Kids Club
- DK Find Out
- Solar System Scope

Use the scales provided in the downloads to support children in making scale models of the planets. The size of the space you have available will dictate the scale chosen. The children then work in groups of ten (eight planets, one Sun and one person to organise everyone) to measure out an approximate scale and place their planets in appropriate places in the scale model.

Once the children acting as the Sun, Mercury, Venus, Earth and Mars are in position, ask the planets to move around the Sun, so that children can see that the planets do not move around in a straight line as often depicted in diagrams. Watching a model such as the one available from Solar Scope will help with this.

Children should use the trundle wheels to continue measuring out their scale model of the solar system. Each child holding a 'planet' should remain stationary until Neptune is in place. The child who is the organiser should then take a photograph.

Ensure that children wash their hands thoroughly after working outdoors.

Assessment for Learning

Ask the children how the planets move. Do any planets move around the Earth? Ask them how scientists in the past learnt that the heliocentric model of the solar system is correct.

Science Capital

Ask the children whether they have seen any planets – several are visible to the naked eye. Do they know the names of any constellations? Find out whether any of the children have seen the International Space Station travelling across the sky at night. Has anyone visited a planetarium? Discuss any recent stories about space that might have been in the news.

Support

Give the children an information sheet that shows the order of planets and their distances from the Sun.

Extension

To add extra challenge for more able children, ask them to work out their own scales based on the real distances between the Sun and the planets.

Follow up

Children could create a scale model of the solar system for a display.

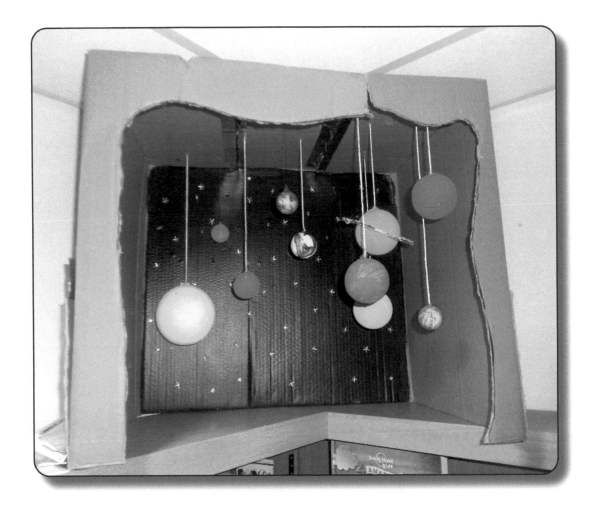

Key vocabulary

Sun, Moon, Mercury, Venus, Earth, Mars, Jupiter, Saturn, Uranus, Neptune, spherical, solar system, rotates, star, orbit, planets

Download resources and links @ www.millgatehouse.co.uk/tpsoresources

23. Forces

Conceptual knowledge

In this activity, children recognise that some mechanisms, including levers, allow a smaller force to have a greater effect.

Working scientifically

In this activity, children report and present findings from enquiries using appropriate scientific language.

Assessment

Children meeting both the conceptual knowledge objective and the working scientifically objective will be able to say or write that it is easier to lift a weight if you push down on the end of a lever.

Activity - Investigating levers

Resources needed

Plank(s) of wood (The seesaw plank must be strong enough for the loads that will be put on it. The wood needs to be smooth so it doesn't cut or splinter a child)
Something to use as a fulcrum or pivot (small log, for example)
Things to use as a weights

What to do

Ask the children about their experience of levers in everyday life. Examples might include using a spoon to open a tin of paint, sitting on a seesaw, cranes and wheelbarrows.

Ask the children how levers benefit us. They change the direction of force and, if you move the pivot or fulcrum, more or less force is needed.

Give the children the opportunity to explore levers for themselves. Provide them with small planks of wood and objects such as bricks that they can lift with the levers. Then ask them to explore what happens when they move the fulcrum or pivot.

Next, provide the children with a longer strong plank of wood and a log to use as a seesaw. Do ensure that this is supervised closely by an adult. Ensure that planks are kept low to minimise risk.

Challenge them to lift a heavier person (such as the teacher).

Children do not need to understand mechanical advantage at this age, but should be able to work out that less effort is required if the distance from the fulcrum, where the force (effort) is applied, is increased.

The children should report or present their findings using vocabulary such as lever, force and effort. This might take the form of a verbal presentation, or might be written up more formally.

Ensure that children wash their hands thoroughly after working outdoors.

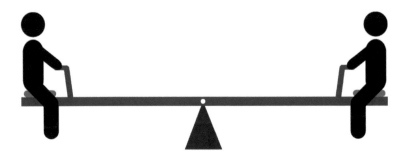

Assessment for Learning

Challenge the children to lift an adult! Can the smallest child lift the adult? Ask them what they would need to do to use less force to lift a heavy weight.

Science Capital

Ask the children where they see or use levers in their everyday lives (e.g. screwdriver or spoon to open a can of paint; nutcracker, etc.) Find out if the people they live with work with levers. Discuss jobs that involve levers, such as mechanic, engineer and architect.

Support

Give the children a frame in which to report their findings (see downloads).

Extension

To add extra challenge for more able children, ask them to choose how to record their findings; ask them to make measurements to contribute towards what they report (for example, they could measure what length of lever is required to lift a particular weight).

Follow up

Ask children to annotate a picture of a lever in action to show how levers allow a smaller force to have a greater effect.

The edge of the tin is the pivot

This is a lever. Because it is longer on this side, you need less effort to lift the lid.

Key vocabulary

Force, mechanisms, simple machines, levers, pivot, fulcrum, effort, load

24. Living things and their habitats

Conceptual knowledge

In this activity, children describe how living things are classified into broad groups according to common observable characteristics and based on similarities and differences, including microorganisms, plants and animals.

Working scientifically

In this activity, children record data and results of increasing complexity using classification keys.

Assessment

Children meeting both the conceptual knowledge objective and the working scientifically objective will be able to create a classification key to identify different microorganisms, plants and animals.

Activity - Creating classification keys

Resources needed

Classification keys / ID books / app for identifying minibeasts
Pooter or container in which to catch minibeasts
Magnifying glasses.

What to do

This lesson should ideally follow lessons in which children have used classification keys to identify different plants and animals.

The children should catch and identify at least 6 different minibeasts using classification keys or identification apps. They then closely observe the minibeasts that they have found, looking for similarities and differences.

Children may find it helpful to photograph the minibeasts.

They then group their minibeasts in different ways (legs or no legs; wings or no wings, etc.) and create their own classification key. This simple classification key, showing some of the common minibeasts in the school grounds, could then be given to younger children to introduce them to using classification keys.

Ensure that children wash their hands thoroughly after working outdoors.

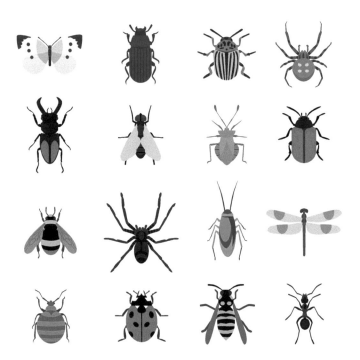

Assessment for Learning

Ask the children what the similarities and differences are between the different minibeasts that they are classifying. Can they describe the characteristics they observe and explain why they have chosen to classify using particular characteristics?

Science Capital

Discuss the children's prior experiences of classifying items; this might include systems for organising toys or stationery. Talk about different STEM careers that involve classifying plants and animals – these might include entomologist, palaeontologist and botanist. Consider asking the children to contribute to a citizen science project.

Support

Children might create a character table to help with creating a classification key (see downloads).

Extension

To add extra challenge for more able children, ask them to classify a larger number of minibeasts.

Follow up

Ask the children to create a number of additional classification keys for different types of microorganisms, plants or animals.

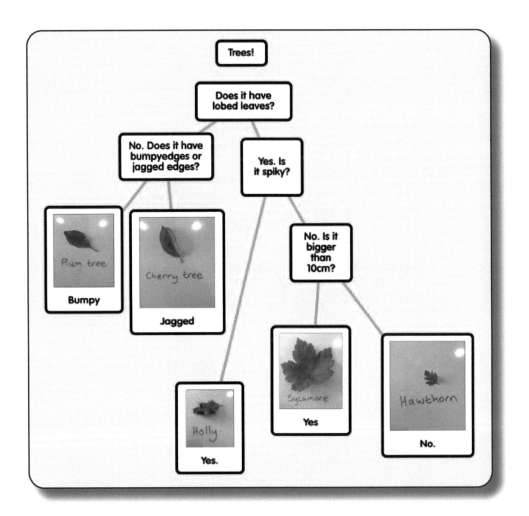

Key vocabulary

Vertebrates, amphibians, invertebrates, insects, spiders, snails, worms, flowering, non-flowering

Download resources and links @ www.millgatehouse.co.uk/tpsoresources

25. Animals including humans

Conceptual knowledge

In this activity, children identify and name the main parts of the human circulatory system, and describe the functions of the heart, blood vessels and blood.

Working scientifically

In this activity, children report and present findings from enquiries.

Assessment

Children meeting the conceptual knowledge objective will be able to represent their understanding of the human circulatory system through environmental art.

Children meeting the working scientifically objective will be able to create a visual representation of the circulatory system, having carried out their own research.

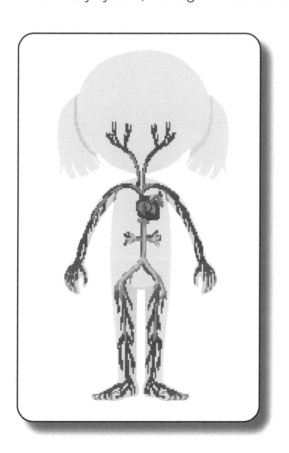

Activity - Modelling the circulatory system

Resources needed

Chalk.
Cards – (blue on one side and red on the other)

What to do

This lesson should ideally follow lessons in which children have had the opportunity to carry out their own research into the circulatory system (see downloads).

Talk to the children about how every part of our body needs blood to keep working. When blood leaves the heart, it contains oxygen. When that same blood returns to the heart, the oxygen has been used up. Explain that they are going to create a model of how the circulatory system works.

Mark out a space on the playground to represent the heart. In this space, there should be a pile of the cards, blue side up (representing deoxygenated blood).

Mark out another space to represent the lungs.

Set up a number of other body parts, e.g. the arms and legs, brain, stomach or eyes. These could be represented by marking out shapes on a playground, or with hula hoops.

The children then act as the blood. They go to the heart and collect a card (blue side up), which they should take to the lungs. There, they turn over the card (red side up) – it has now been oxygenated. They then return to the heart with the oxygenated blood. Next, they take the card to one of the other body parts and turn it over as it is now deoxygenated (blue side up). They then return to the heart and repeat the process. Periodically pause and discuss what is happening, address any misconceptions.

Finally the children use either natural materials or chalk to make a visual representation of the circulatory system. They should now be able to describe how the circulatory system works.

Ensure that children wash their hands thoroughly after working outdoors.

Assessment for Learning

Children could recount the journey of a blood cell – this could even be done as a drama activity. This provides many opportunities to identify misconceptions and address in future teaching.

Science Capital

Sensitively explore children's personal experiences – do any of the children know someone with a heart problem? Do they know what has caused this? Discuss blood donation with children – this could be an opportunity to share your own experiences or to ask a parent to share theirs. Talk about different careers that involve knowledge of the circulatory system. These might include doctors, paramedics and nurses. Consider engaging with organisations such as 'Medical Mavericks' which promote careers in the NHS for schoolchildren.

Support

Provide children with a diagram of the circulatory system (see downloads).

Extension

To add extra challenge for more able children, ask them to create a more detailed model of the circulatory system, including the capillaries, veins and arteries.

Follow up

Ask the children to create a labelled diagram of the circulatory system.

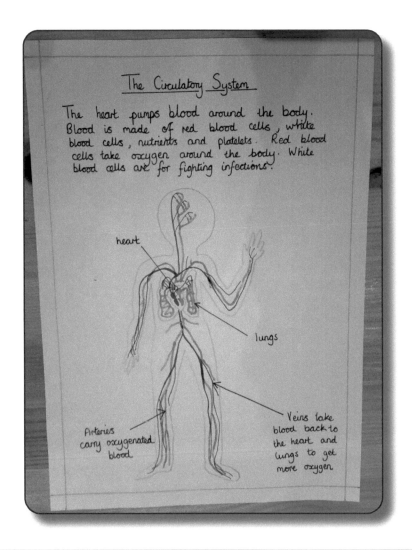

Key vocabulary

Heart, pulse, rate, pumps, blood, blood vessels, transported, lungs, oxygen, carbon dioxide, nutrients, water, muscles, cycle, circulatory system, organs, flow

26. Evolution and inheritance

Conceptual knowledge

In this activity, children identify how animals and plants are adapted to suit their environment in different ways and recognise that adaptation may lead to evolution.

Working scientifically

In this activity, children record data and results of increasing complexity using tables.

Assessment

Children meeting the conceptual knowledge objective will be able to describe how camouflage is one way in which animals and plants are adapted to suit their environment.

Children meeting the working scientifically objective will be able to record their findings about the locations and minibeasts in a table.

Activity - Exploring camouflage as an adaptation

Resources needed

Pooters (ensure that poopers are cleaned/disinfected before and after use)
Magnifying glasses
Pots for minibeasts
Minibeast identification sheets or books
Pencil and paper or tablet
80+ short (10 cm) pieces of wool in at least 4 different colours (one colour should match the ground colour)

What to do

Discuss the children's understanding of the term 'adaptation'. Can they give examples of adaptation?

Adaptation is the biological mechanism by which organisms adjust to new environments or to changes in their current environment. Adaptation leads to evolution. Camouflage is one example of adaptation.

Ask the children to search for minibeasts. They should look closely at them for evidence of camouflage. Discuss why many of the minibeasts that they have found are camouflaged.

The children then create a table to show which minibeasts were found in which locations and what the colour of the minibeast was. Can they find a link between the number of minibeasts found in each location and the colour of the minibeast?

Play a quick game of 'Camouflage Worms' with the children. Scatter the pieces of wool around a given area. Tell the children that they are now birds and that they need to eat the 'worms'. Split the children into teams. Each team member should collect one piece of wool – relay style. After a short period of time, stop the game and compare which coloured 'worms' have been 'eaten' and which have survived. Talk about how those 'worms' that survived would go on to produce offspring with the same traits, ensuring that they too have a better chance of survival.

Ensure that children wash their hands thoroughly after working outdoors.

Assessment for Learning

Ask the children why they think animals might be camouflaged. Children could look at three minibeasts and discuss which is the odd one out and why.

Science Capital

Discuss the children's experiences of camouflage – they may have camouflaged clothes or a parent in the military who wears camouflaged clothes. Tell the children about any local nature sites that they could visit – or, better yet, arrange a class trip! Talk about STEM professionals who might need to know about adaptation such as entomologists, ecologists and zoologists.

Support

Provide the children with a frame in which to record their findings (see downloads).

Extension

To add extra challenge for more able children, ask them to explore what benefits there are in not being camouflaged – some animals are brightly coloured as a warning to predators that they are poisonous. This can be explored in the game of 'Camouflage Worms': tell the children that the red worms are poisonous – what effect will this have on the behaviour of the 'birds'?

Follow up

Children could research other adaptations that animals have.

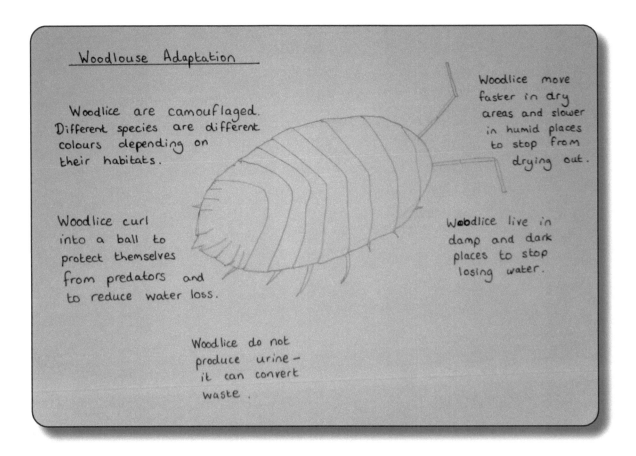

Woodlouse Adaptation

Woodlice are camouflaged. Different species are different colours depending on their habitats.

Woodlice move faster in dry areas and slower in humid places to stop from drying out.

Woodlice curl into a ball to protect themselves from predators and to reduce water loss.

Woodlice live in damp and dark places to stop losing water.

Woodlice do not produce urine – it can convert waste.

Key vocabulary

Offspring, vary, characteristics, suited, adapted, environment, inherited, species, camouflage

27. Light

Conceptual knowledge

In this activity, children recognise that light appears to travel in straight lines.

Working scientifically

In this activity, children report explanations in oral and written forms.

Assessment

Children meeting the conceptual knowledge objective will be able to model or explain how light travels in straight lines.

Children meeting the working scientifically objective will be able to explain how light travels in straight lines, orally or in a written format.

Activity - Modelling light travelling in straight lines

Resources needed

Small mirrors
Natural materials or chalk
Lengths of ribbon
Objects to look at (these could be found objects such as fir cones, or things like cuddly toys),
torches (these do not need to work!)

What to do

This lesson should be one of the first taught in this topic.

Start by discussing with the children what they already know about light. They should already know that light is reflected from surfaces and that we need light in order to see things. Ask the children to represent how they see objects. They can use natural materials or chalk for this task. This provides an excellent opportunity to address any misconceptions.

Give out small mirrors and ask the children if they can see behind them using the mirrors. How do they think this happens? Remind them not to look directly at the Sun, even via a mirror. Ask children if they can represent this in chalk or using natural materials.

Children should then model how light travels in straight lines, using ribbon. This may need to be modelled to children first. Ensure that children wash their hands thoroughly after working outdoors.

Children should be asked to orally explain how light travels in straight lines either to each other or to an audience – you could potentially ask the children to explain and model how light travels in straight lines to younger children who will also be learning about light.

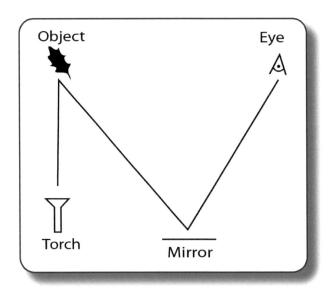

Assessment for Learning

Ask the children to represent their understanding of how light travels using natural materials or chalk.

Science Capital

Ask the children whether they have used periscopes before. There may be local light show events that can be discussed with children. Share with the children ideas about how they might make a periscope at home with their families. Discuss STEM professionals who need to know about the way in which light travels. These might include performing arts engineers, astronauts and film production engineers.

Support

Provide children with an image to show how we see things (see downloads).

Extension

To add extra challenge for more able children, ask them to model what would happen if multiple mirrors were used – modelling how a periscope works.

Follow up

Children could write an explanation of how light travels in straight lines.

LIGHT

Light travels in straight lines. Light does not come out of our eyes. People used to foolishly think that it did a long time ago, but now they know that it doesn't. Light comes from a light source like the bright sun. It travels in a straight line in all directions. When light hits an object, like a toy bear, it reflects. It reflects into our eyes. If there is a mirror, or other reflective surface (glass or water are good examples) light can reflect off this too which can let people see round corners.

Key vocabulary

Straight lines, light, light source, dark, absence of light, shiny, matt, surface, reflect, mirror, sunlight, dangerous

28. Electricity

Conceptual knowledge

In this activity, children use recognised symbols when representing a simple circuit in a diagram.

Working scientifically

In this activity, children plan different types of scientific enquiries to answer questions and take measurements, using data loggers.

Assessment

Children meeting the conceptual knowledge objective will be able to mark out a circuit diagram to show how their solar powered fan works.

Children meeting the working scientifically objective will be able to take readings on a data logger and plan a pattern-seeking investigation.

Activity - Using recognised circuit symbols

Resources needed

Data loggers or other lux meters
Child-made solar powered fans (make sure that the fans are low power so they can't cause injury from the rotating blades)
Chalk, pencil and paper or tablet

What to do

This lesson should follow a lesson, or series of lessons, in which children make solar powered fans (see downloads for various examples).

Ask the children to draw a circuit diagram of their fan using the correct symbols in chalk on the playground.

Using their own solar powered fans, the children plan and carry out a pattern-seeking investigation to find out whether more sunlight (measured in lux) is associated with a faster-moving fan. They need to use use data loggers or lux meters to find out how much sunlight there is. Unless the fans are turning very slowly, and rotations can be counted accurately, children will only be able to observe whether fans are turning quickly or slowly.

Ensure that children wash their hands thoroughly after working outdoors.

Assessment for Learning

Ask the children what the different circuit symbols mean. Ask what would happen if there were gaps in the circuit, or if any of the components were replaced.

Science Capital

Ask the children about their experiences of electricity and circuits. They may have electricity sets at home, or may have helped to wire a plug. Find out if any of the children have family members who work as electricians – perhaps a parent could come in and talk to the children about their job. Arrange a visit to a local power station or take part in a virtual tour.

Support

Give children a frame in which to record results (see downloads).

Extension

To add extra challenge for more able children, ask them to come up with their own additional questions to investigate, considering things such as whether the direction that the solar panel is pointing affects the speed of the fan.

Follow up

Children could be asked to draw circuit diagrams to represent pictorial diagrams or physical circuits.

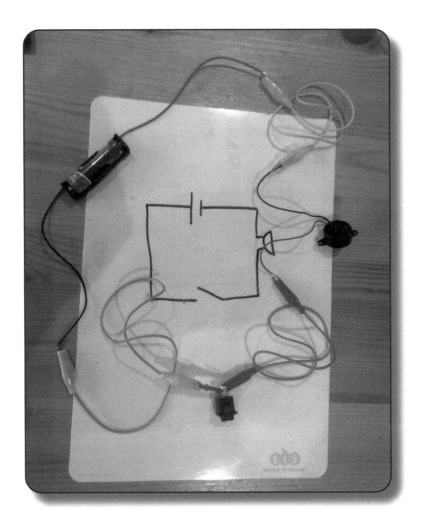

Key vocabulary

Circuit, complete circuit, circuit diagram, circuit symbol, cell, battery, bulb, buzzer, motor, switch

Taking outdoor learning further

To further develop outdoor learning in your school, consider some of the following ideas:

- Read back through the introduction. Consider why you want to develop outdoor learning. Just as with teaching indoors, outdoor learning needs to be effectively planned for. This means being clear about why learning is taking place in a particular environment, how curriculum objectives are going to be covered and how all children are going to be supported so that they have the opportunity to succeed.

- Take a copy of your curriculum or long-term plan. In green, highlight the objectives or statements that **should** be taught outdoors, or are easily taught outdoors. For primary science, these are likely to be those that involve identifying plants and trees or learning about habitats. In yellow, highlight other objectives or statements that could be taught outdoors. Depending on your starting point, you might want to make sure that all of the green statements are taught outdoors, or you might want to start work on the yellow statements.

- Attend **Professional Development** about teaching primary science outdoors.

- Visit other schools that have prioritised outdoor learning and find out how they have embedded these practices.

- Support your colleagues to develop their skills in teaching primary science outdoors. Consider trying some of the activities in this book at a staff meeting. There is an excellent structure for a staff meeting on the PLAN Assessment website.

- Discuss outdoor learning with your Senior Leadership Team – explore whether targets relating to teaching outdoors could be included in the School Development Plan.

References

Dowdell, K., Gray, T. & Malone, K. (2011). 'Nature and its influence on children's outdoor play', *Australian Journal of Outdoor Education*, 15, (2), pp. 24–35.

Education Endowment Foundation (2021). *Education Endowment Foundation*. Available from: https://educationendowmentfoundation.org.uk/evidence-summaries/teaching-learning-toolkit/outdoor-adventure-learning/ [Accessed 03/01/21].

Engemann, K., Pedersen, C., Arge, L., Tsirogiannis, C., Mortensen, P. and Svenning, J. (2019). Residential green space in childhood is associated with lower risk of psychiatric disorders from adolescence into adulthood. *Proceedings of the National Academy of Sciences*. 116(11). Available at: https://www.pnas.org/content/116/11/5188 [Accessed 08/04/21].

Hamilton, J. (2018). *Outdoor Learning: closing the attainment gap in primary schoolchildren in Scotland*. Dumfries: Forest Research. Available at: https://www.forestresearch.gov.uk/research/outdoor-learning-closing-the-attainment-gap-in-primary-schoolchildren-in-scotland/ [Accessed: 03/01/2021].

Harlen, W. and Qualter, A. (2014). *The Teaching of Science in Primary Schools*. Oxon: Routledge.

Harvey, M., Rankine, K. and Jensen, R. (2017). Outdoor Learning Hubs: A Scottish Attainment Challenge Innovation Fund Project. [online]. Available from: https://www.sapoe.org.uk/wp-content/uploads/2018/01/Outdoor-Hub-Learning-Report-Dec-2017-V1.pdf [Accessed 3 Jan 2021].

Hoath, L. (2015). *A framework for understanding the distinctive characteristics of an outdoor setting pedagogy: a comparative primary education case study approach*. Doctoral thesis, Sheffield Hallam University. Available at: http://shura.shu.ac.uk/18459/ [Accessed 3 Jan 2021].

Ofsted (2008) *Learning outside the classroom: How far should you go?* [online]. Available at: https://www.lotc.org.uk/wp-content/uploads/2010/12/Ofsted-Report-Oct-2008.pdf [Accessed 09/04/2021].

Twohig-Bennett, C, and Jones, A. (2018). The health benefits of the great outdoors: A systematic review and meta-analysis of greenspace exposure and health outcomes. *Environmental Research*. 166 (October 2018), Pages 628-637. Available at: https://www.sciencedirect.com/science/article/pii/S0013935118303322 [Accessed 03/01/21].

Waite, S., Passy, R., Gilchrist, M., Hunt, A. & Blackwell, I. (2016). *Natural Connections Demonstration Project, 2012-2016: Final Report. Natural England Commissioned Reports, Number 215*. York: Natural England. Available from: http://publications.naturalengland.org.uk/publication/6636651036540928 [Accessed 3 Jan 2021].